MW01644757

Philip Dacey | *The Ice-Cream Vigils*

Previous Collections of Poems by Philip Dacey

*How I Escaped From the Labyrinth and Other Poems* (Carnegie-Mellon U. Press, 1977)

*The Boy Under the Bed* (The Johns Hopkins U. Press, 1981)

*Gerard Manley Hopkins Meets Walt Whitman in Heaven and Other Poems* (Penmaen, 1982)

*The Man With Red Suspenders* (Milkweed Editions, 1986)
*Night Shift at the Crucifix Factory* (U. of Iowa Press, 1991)

*The Deathbed Playboy* (Eastern Washington U. Press, 1999)

*The Paramour of the Moving Air* (Quarterly Review of Literature, 1999)

*The Mystery of Max Schmitt: Poems on the Life and Work of Thomas Eakins* (Turning Point Books, 2004)

*The New York Postcard Sonnets: A Midwesterner Moves to Manhattan* (Rain Mountain Press, 2007)

*Vertebrae Rosaries: 50 Sonnets* (Red Dragonfly Press, 2009)

*Mosquito Operas: New and Selected Short Poems* (Rain Mountain Press, 2010)

*Gimme Five* (Blue Light Press, 2013)

*Church of the Adagio* (Rain Mountain Press, 2016)

Philip Dacey

# THE ICE-CREAM VIGILS: LAST POEMS

Red Dragonfly Press

ISBN 978-1-945063-08-4

Library of Congress Control Number: 2016955989

Full acknowledgments printed at back of book

Cover Art: 'Cloud Ladder' by Doug Johnson

Designed and typeset by Scott King
using Dante MT Std (text) & Carter Sans (titles)

Published by Red Dragonfly Press
P. O. Box 98
Northfield, MN 55057
www.reddragonflypress.org

# Author's Note

The "last" in the subtitle refers not only to recent poems, written since the previous book, but also to earlier ones published in journals over the years but not yet included in a collection of my work. Some of that large category seemed to warrant recycling and a place here, but given my culpable productivity and the plethora of choices facing me, I decided to help myself by limiting the book to 50 poems, an arbitrary number but no more arbitrary than fourteen lines to a poem. The book was completed as I entered the final stages of my experience with leukemia. A special thank you to Scott King for his interest in the project.

# Table of Contents

for Ingrid Ines

*Welcome!*

# OPENING ACTS

## 1. First Memory

I'm standing in a crib, my head
just above the railing, which I grip
as I look down onto the bed
where my parents fight, who will not stop

despite all my loud crying meant
to get them to do just that. Am I three?
Maybe only two. The argument
does not end before my memory,

nor do I drop to the mattress and return
to sleep. Throughout, my hands grip the cool
railing, cool even while the burn
of words acts like a lesson in some school.

Did my parents never die? Is it true
they are still fighting, and I am still two?

### 2. Bic

Eighth grade. Study hour. I'm in a front-row desk,
just a few feet from Sr. Mary Rose,
who's grading tests. As I read, I idly flick
my pen, which slips from my fingers and flies

end-over-end straight for the crown of thorns
stitched in red like a bull's-eye on the breast
of her black habit and hits home, point-first,
startling her as it falls to her lap and my face burns.

I rise to retrieve the missile and apologize.
Sister, who gingerly picks up and holds out
to me the offending weapon, smiles and says,
as if there were no accidents, "Good shot,"

leaving me hanging conflicted on a cross,
equally proud and ashamed of my success.

# FAMILY STORIES

## I. For Aunt Mary, Who Jumped

My brother, a policeman, got the call
to come identify the body on
the street after Aunt Mary jumped. The sill
she launched from, five floors up, was a white line

past which my brother's partner poked his head
to say no accident, he'd found a note.
Few words. Why live, with Uncle Russell dead?
My brother never spoke about the sight.

Did Mary stand or sit or kneel before
she let go of everything solid at the last
and wrote herself forever on the air?
Of all the aunts, the sweetest, funniest.

Whenever I think of her, she jumps again
and mocks this poem, which reaches for her in vain.

## 2. Elegy: A Rondel for Bernard

My uncle Bernard froze off all his toes
sleeping under a bridge in wintry Detroit.
How things came to that, I've never figured out:
his warmth and wit were always my good news.

"Homeless" wasn't then the word people would use;
Grandpa called him a bum, said, "Get out of my sight."
My uncle Bernard froze off all his toes
sleeping under a bridge in wintry Detroit.

My mother tried to steer him straight. Who knows
what might have helped him find a different route?
I think of the snow, the cold, the way the night
covered him as all roads began to close.
My uncle Bernard froze off all his toes.

# IN PRAISE OF CHINESE POTTERY

The relationship between
this chill vase
and the scurry
and inarticulate
stammer of survival.

The heat of
panic: no form
bears it. Yet
a life struck
and set this

vase, relieved
itself of a hard, tight
pressure—an
encroachment on
space and breath.

Taken in to
its shape, the
energy and pursuit
of a destroyer; fixed
there in

cherry glaze,
a stay from
fear. The loss
impending but
mute now and in colors.

## THE PIANO

"The piano is not in the right place."
– overheard at a recital

The piano sank
into the grave
of my mother,
whom the keys miss.

The piano is inside the ripest berry,
the sounds of black and white
swelling to red.

The piano has entered the sun
for re-charging.

The piano rose tonight
into the constellation Piano.

The piano has gone to the bank
to deposit its history of notes.

The piano now lives atop
a tall pillar in the desert
with St. Simeon and the Stylites.
Pilgrims wonder at
the black hulk against the sky.

The piano is nesting
in someone's thick, long hair,
hatching the eros of ivory.

The piano is always in the right place.

# THE D MINOR ORGAN TOCCATA AND FUGUE

The audience for Bach was old and white
And looking monied, too, pew after pew.
The air of privilege was everywhere.

But the Master's notes, innocent of the sight
Of age, color, class, did just what they'd come to do—
Distribute their gifts equally, ear by ear.

# SHOWER: A TRIOLET

When did I stop singing in the shower?
Did something of mine run down the drain?
I soap myself just as I did before,
but, still, I've stopped singing in the shower.
Did my songs weaken slowly hour by hour
or burst like bubbles in all this soapy rain?
When did I stop? Singing in the shower,
I must have not seen what ran down the drain.

# O, DAD, UNTIE THE KNOT!

O, Dad, untie the knot!
And I untie the knot,
thinking of knots
knotting themselves

against all fine fingers,
the knots beautiful
in their complexity,
think first, and last,

of the knot of love,
pulled fast beyond
undoing, knowing,
all of us at its center,

breathing; the knot
of not, of what
fails to be, and this one
we cannot see,

cannot find to unwind,
our fingers disappear
in the search; the knot
of blood, the thick

red ropes
in each other's arms,
like lovers or wrestlers
to a death; and the knot

of the idea of knots,
twisting in the brain
to snag us.
                                        There,
it's undone. Now, Son,

the other shoe. What,
there is no knot there?
Why, what shall we do?
Whatever shall we do?

# WALKING THE PICKET LINE WITH THE GHOSTS OF HIS FATHER AND GRANDFATHER

Ghosts are coming out of
all our mouths this fall dawn
and mixing with steam from coffee
sympathizers have placed in our hands.

One citizen, either not yet awake
or else angry at our nerve,
guns his car through the crosswalk,
narrowly missing a picketer.

Only I can see the two men
who carry my name carrying their
insubstantial signs
as they weave among their brothers,

going nose to nose with each
to study the lineaments of care,
the same lineaments etched
in faces decades earlier.

This is a first for my grandfather,
whose bosses in the coalmine
in southern Illinois would rather
have killed than allow a union,

though my father walked the line
in front of the gates at McDonnell
Aircraft in St. Louis, his lifetime
employer, who learned to treat him well.

A first for me, too, with my stick
and cardboard, high-fives, the gab
of jokes and local politics,
and peering into cars for scabs.

Now the sun, completely above
the horizon, moves in step
with us, who vote to give
it honorary union membership.

And the ghosts have come to stand
on either side of me. I swear
I feel sheltered by them from the wind
starting to rise, like a wage that's fair.

# ZOOT: A RONDEL

In '42, Los Angeles banned the zoot suit.
Crime came woven into the clothes some wore.
A zoot suit was all you'd need to start a war:
"Tell me what you wear, and I'll tell you if you shoot."

Zoot-suited gangs incited foes to riot.
A zoot suit said, "It's time to settle the score."
In '42 Los Angeles banned the zoot suit.
The city's peace hung from the clothes you wore.

Baggy pants and a flamboyant long coat—
didn't the Huns wear something similar?
Our brave boys overseas were dressed in gore.
Get into a uniform or else salute.
In '42, Los Angeles banned the zoot suit.

# SARATOGA SPRINGS (New York)

Oh, it was beautiful, the horses working out
at dawn, silhouettes against the sun
and eating up the track for breakfast
while I ate up the glamour of the place
and one especial combination slowing
toward me, of a female jockey and a great
red stallion snorting out the morning
in clouds, the woman's hair upcurling
from beneath her cap, her face Grecian
in the light as she leaned against
his straining neck, her face beside
the greater face, her lips beside
an ear and moving, spilling secrets
to the beast, and I imagined
what she whispered there, about her love
for him and how he flowed in strength,
about her need to feel his mane the length
of her adoring face, and how the two
of them were one, until they neared
my post enough, that overwhelming pair,
for me to hear precisely what
it was she had to say, who I was sure
was purest thankfulness that he should be,
and these words softly split the day:
"Don't you pull any of that shit on me."

# TWO NEW YORK SONGS

## I. Song of the Hat Vendor (Columbus Avenue)

Let others struggle to change themselves;
    Your new self fits in your hands.
I've hats with feathers and some with wide brims
    And some with red velvet bands.

Come let a grey bowler banish your past,
    Or a tam or cloche or beret.
Simply pull this beauty snug to your ears,
    And your history starts today.

With the flash of a hand to your head, gone
    Is the person you used to be.
This derby—tilt it!—tells all in your path
    You're one who's living free.

Try straw? Now hold up the mirror to know
    Just how the new you looks.
Where else could such easy transformation
    Be had for so few bucks?

You, Sir, you Madam—stop a minute
    To try this on for size.
Its feel may match your secret dream,
    And you win yourself as prize.

## 2. Manhattan Song

Let one of my heavens be
the pedestrian island
at 80th and Broadway,
where I will be found

at some eternal noon
reading a book
on a bench in the sun
as on both sides the traffic

flows and walkers cross
in front of me.
Motion and stasis.
I'll have become T.

S. Eliot's still point
of the turning world, unless
a still point can't
also sip the bless-

ing of a coffee
from Zabar's.
And let Gabriel be
the man at the far

end of the bench who,
as if in his room all alone,
blows on an alto
sax a sweet, sad tune.

# "WHAT DO YOU MISS MOST ABOUT NEW YORK CITY?"

The island within an island—Central Park
(constructed nature) nested in Manhattan
(hardly a deserted one). Dog-walkers with a fan
of breeds coming behind like a ship's wake.

Overhearing the music of Hebrew on my block,
(thank you, Synagogue). Yarmulkes and brownstones
wherever I look. Being first in line,
me junkie, at Juilliard, where students rock.

The subway, best possible church, all the intimate
strangers, crowded, face-to-face—grace
abounding. The view of downtown, walking across
the Brooklyn Bridge—faerie castles. Friends, like Colette.

The Fairway, where grocery shopping's a contact sport.
And everywhere a U. N. of voices, peaceful consort.

# CITY: ON THE PHOTOGRAPHY OF DOUG JOHNSON

Mill City Clinic Gallery, Minneapolis

Boxes, lit from within and without, soar.
Trapped in verticals, the ghost of a face.
Even the grid can't hold the sun in place.
Say what? To build a city out of flour.

A chorus of speed—headlights elongate to tongues.
Old brick, old lettering, but—look!—new eyes.
Windows like cartoon squares: the office comedies.
Infernal sunset—which of Dante's rings?

Architectural forms—characters in a story;
here, framed and hung, studies of the plot.
Upside down, an entire city can float.
Night colors on the water: hallucinatory.
For vertigo, stare upwards at a bank.
At riverside, the city stoops to drink.

# FEDERICO FELLINI AT LAKE CALHOUN, MINNEAPOLIS

Beside the path beside the lake, an accordionist.
The music of Nino Rota fills the air.
Fellini in Minnesota? Who could have guessed?

Dan the Accordion Man is back and not to be missed.
His hat's upturned atop the carrying case—show you care.
Beside the path beside the lake, an accordionist

turns the circling summertime crowd into a cast
of characters in a Fellini film, the soundtrack a Rota score.
Italy in Lutheranland. Who could have guessed?

Draped Somali women, undraped bikinied teens, and the rest—
bikers, runners, skateboarders, rollerbladers—each a star
on la strada beside the lake. Ciao, Accordionist!

It's *La Dolce Vita* Twin Cities-style. Put in a request:
the theme from *Amarcord*, or *8½*, and the ear
gives thanks to Nino, Federico, and Dan. Who can resist?

Absent Marcello Mastroianni, let Sven Olsen be kissed
on screen—in the movie we're in as we watch it—here
beside the path beside the lake, as an accordionist
welcomes Fellini to Minneapolis. Who could have guessed?

# THE BUZZ

I watch the clock, but when it's time
to start the class I hesitate.
I've fallen in love again with the hum
of voices, students deep in a chat.

On the shore of their heedless ocean,
low roar of easy tete-a-tetes
free from my bell-like "Let's begin,"
I fake-fuss with a stack of notes.

Weeks ago, at the start of the term,
they sat, mostly strangers, silent,
but now they've formed a kind of team,
veterans of the poetry front.

Or else poetry is what they are,
their voices anyway, beyond
translation, sense no more than blur,
words in service of pure sound.

Now it's one minute, now it's two
past the hour, and still I can't bear
to throttle this community.
How long can I dumbly stand here?

Some students start watching me
watching them talk and wonder what's up:
they know I take my job seriously,
that, as teacher, I play for keeps.

But what I want to keep is them,
their insouciance, like Whitman's animals.
Here's to the view from the podium!
Then duty demurs: break the spell.

I could tell them what I've seen, heard,
or take roll, talk assignments, due dates.
Instead I start to read outloud
as someone sitting by himself might,

near sotto voce, underground stream
feeding in to their general stir:
"Had we but world enough and time..."
They quiet, to catch what's on the air.

# LETTER TO THOMAS McGRATH

I

Robert Bly asked the dead sparrow in his hand
to forgive him for all the hours spent
listening to the radio. Tom, I ask you to forgive me
for all the hours I did not hold your books in my hands.

In 1970 I even betrayed you.
Charged with the task—privilege—of taking the reins
of your returning *Crazy Horse*
and fresh out of Iowa's writing mill,
I put into that stallion's feedbag the dope of mainstream careerism
and drugged the madness out of him, corporatized
his heroic body.
Mussolini: "Fascism should have been called 'corporatism.'"
Forgive me for that, too.

You said Cal (not Lowell, oh not Lowell) the farmhand
led you to the light but you were too young to enter.
Whenever our paths crossed in Minnesota,
I was too young (culpably so) to enter your light.
Now I miss the conversations we didn't have.

I would have told you of my Irish grandfathers,
the one killed young by his coalmine work
in Southern Illinois in 1900, the other at the same time
excoriating in verse the English in New York's Irish Times.
You, a master curser, boiler of language
over the flame of anger till the pot jumps off the stove,
its scalding syllables flying in all directions,

and believer with Mohammed Dib that
"Nothing is more a sacrament than a curse,"
would have cursed all oppressors everywhere.

And I would have asked about your working on the docks
in Manhattan's Chelsea district, the year I was born.
I went there yesterday to look for your ghost studying
the cries of flying gulls,
but found only the Chelsea Piers, a sports
and entertainment mall. You would not be surprised,
you who no less than Lorca
breathed fire on New York,
he there ten years before you: I want your ghosts
to meet on a bench in Washington Square Park
and passersby to see tiny flame-flakes
where your words dart back and forth between you,
neither Spanish nor English but the language of healing fire.

II

When you sing in high gear,
your X-treme wordmongering and verbal foliation
a form of High Blarney, an aural Book of Kells,
the wind listens and takes notes, reshapes itself
to blow with greater color.

Your six-gun tongue came riding out of the West,
the pain of history's loss translated into
a blazing barrel, an arsenal of waves in the ear.

You were Joycean on a threshing machine, harvesting words.

At the junction of dream and reality,
your Irish gab twisted and turned in the prison
of the barbed world, left elaborate patterns of sound
like star charts on the air.

III

More than thirty years after the war
killed your brother, you were unable to read
"Blues for Jimmy" in public.
You always wrote out of streaming open wounds, like
multiple mouths.

And the wars continue.
Once again we must
"steam the blood from the dollar bills."

I know your heart burst
deep inside the earth
when Paul Wellstone's plane went down.

And your love for Tomasito
still makes wave crash against the shore.

You promised: "I'll take you, my darlings, over the river
if you open your eyes and slip your foot out of the stone."
It's clear to us all now: you are the Dakotas' Whitman,
the pair of you hand-in-hand
leading us forward on the open road.

## THE PUGILISTS

The aging black man at the Y came out
of the boxing room and held a glove up to me:
"I could use a favor. Would you help me put
this on? These gloves are brand-new. With my free

hand I got on the other, but now I'm stuck."
I pushed, but he soon gave way; he was small.
Then he leaned against the wall to brace his back.
"Push harder. You won't hurt me." I used all

my strength and grunted. We were face-to-face,
inches from each other. "My thumb's almost there."
We shoved closer, prizefighters in an embrace.
"That's it. You've done it. Thanks." I joked, "Don't floor

me now with a punch." He swung wide, laughed. Was it
a draw? A win on points? Call it a kind of knockout

## BLACK AND WHITE

St. Louis. The Forties. The neighborhood poor white.
(Or say white trash, given how when the flight
to the suburbs happened muddy lawns greened
all up and down the block, and newly black-owned
homes soon saw their values rocket upward.)
I'm five, playing in the sandbox in our backyard,
when a black child, a boy my age, appears
from out of the alley, sees me, stops and stares.
(Could this be the first such face-to-face
up-close encounter with the other race
for both of us? And how did he come to be there?
His mother a cleaning-woman, and he came with her
until he wandered off, bored watching her dust?)
Suddenly I'm a host and he's my guest.
I gesture toward the sandbox. "Do you want to play?"
A wary look, then he decides to stay.
Little talk. A shared scoop and pail. To build
together, sand on sand. Holes dug, holes filled.
A brotherhood of work a child can do.
Call it a dream. An oasis in time. Call it true.

Enter Mrs. Blandford—the point of this story—
one yard over, a figure of hysteria
on her back porch, waving her arms as she screams
at the boy to get out and stay out and seems
about to charge down her steps just as he
jumps up and scatters sand and dignity
to escape back into the alley, while I,
all wonder, as if lightning had split a blue sky,

don't think to say—too young to have such sense—
"Our yards are separated by a fence
and what happens here is not your business,"
but instead sit still, beginning to score the loss
into memory, so that even long decades away
Mrs. Blandford will burn as fiercely as on that day.

# NOT ABOUT PIE THIEVES

This was going to be a poem about
pie thieves, one of them my father,
but when he saw the poem he said,
I don't like that word "thief"
and I don't like that word "stole."

And I had so wanted to write it,
to tell you how in World War One,
a boy, he lied about his age and joined
the Navy, and how the cook on board
my father's battleship let steaming pies

cool on the galley's window ledge,
as good as home, or better, for this
orphan out to find his, who overcome
by fumes of baked apple and sugar
joined a buddy in a sneak attack

so successful the spoils were one pie apiece
and sweet groans in a dark corner of the ship.
I loved my father's acting like the boy
he was on that gleaming weapon
of destruction he was there to help man.

But he was adamant and thought "take"
would be as good as "stole" nor felt
the compliment in "my father the pie thief,"
until I surrendered with reassurances
I would not use those words, not write that poem.

Now, as my father, sweet old man,
sits on his ledge somewhere
steaming with age and memory,
and Death, who's lied as usual to get on board,
lurks by the window dreaming of feasts,

I have written not that poem but this one,
that asks for forgiveness
for telling a story by not telling it,
for stealing something good that lay
within easy reach and making it mine

to make it yours, for eating the words
of this poem about a poem (including, kiss
of peace, "my son the story thief"), this love
about a love, this pie about a death
so sweet we all want to steal it forever.

# FLY

I caught a fly inside a glass
    I'd set against the wall
and under which I slid a piece
    of paper as a seal,

then took them all—glass, paper, fly—
    out to the balcony
to give the one I'd trapped a chance
    to resume a fly's life, free—

if that's the word for such a one,
    who seemed to like the glass
until I shook it and so forced
    upon him his release,

although I knew I couldn't say
    for sure I wasn't caught
in my own glass, minus the benefit
    of some hand shaking me out.

# THE ANSWER

> "I cannot keep from answering a letter."
> – Donald Hall, on a postcard

You told me not to answer,
that there was no need for me to answer,
but as you can see here I am
answering. I cannot not answer.
Otherwise, how would you know I received
your letter telling me I needn't answer?
I didn't want you to be waiting for me not to answer.
Now you know I am not answering
in the only way I know how
not to.
Feel free yourself not to receive this
if you do not want to answer.

Sometimes not answering
is the best answer.
An answer usually leaves
so much unanswered,
whereas no answer
answers everything,
don't you think? (Don't answer that.)

Still, it must take a saint
to keep from answering a letter,
to let go of the need to answer,
to surrender oneself to that Other
with no postal address, Who of course

always answers by not answering.
Maybe if we asked that One,
who won't even answer which sex It is,
not to answer
instead of always begging for answers
we'd get something in return
besides silence,
which is more of an answer
than we care to have.

For surely it's when we insist we don't need an answer
that we need one more than ever.

Please don't answer.
I will be waiting
not to hear from you.

# THE GOOD GREY POET

## 1. Leaves of Lucre

Walt, I have been thinking about money.
Forgive me.

I laid myself down in the drawer of a cash register
as if it were a manger of swaddling bills.

I held the dollar sign above my mouth
and squeezed it
to live on its juice.

I thought I saw the open road
in a column of numbers.

Nowhere in a landscape of zeroes
could I find your white beard.

Not once did the butterflies Lorca saw circling your head
alight on the coins I had polished and polished
like someone masturbating.

This offer came to me:
Trade the sunlight
for a stash of gold.
And I was ready to.

I would make my life an abstraction
inside a scaffold of decimal points.

I stored my blood deep in a bank vault
and hoped it would accrue interest

I thought if I hung large enough numbers around my neck,
I would fly.

For every plus sign,
a barbaric yawp!

But a nightmare has always recurred:
a minus sign lengthens till it loops
around my neck and pulls tight.

Walt, I confess
I took a green-faced man
in an oval frame
as my camerado.

### 2. Walt and Joe

Until I learned that my father was bisexual,
I had never thought of associating him
with Walt Whitman. It had always been easier
connecting my mother to the poet—she'd have fit in
at Pfaff's, playing piano for all the revelers
as she did at parties in our apartment,
and wasn't Whitman the mother of us all?

But now I see that my father,
uneducated, a laborer, no more bookish

than the tradesmen and mechanics Whitman loved,
could have been one of his roughs—
though a gentle, sweet one—
on the Brooklyn docks.

In the picture of my father and his navy buddy,
both of them in uniform, heads close together,
I want that discoloration in the background
to be not the work of time
but the ghost of the poet,
an emanation like a blessing on these thoughts.

And because I believe that Whitman, who said
he met strangers in the street and loved them,
would have loved my father if he had met him,
I hereby take my father's hand and place it in Walt's
to introduce them: Walt, Joe; Pop, Walt.

Let them talk of mothers—
Whitman's beloved one, my orphaned father's
dead before he could remember her—
and war—the Civil and the First World wars.
And maybe my father says something of me,
how he feared my education would separate us
though it never did.

And now they are sleeping together, arms
thrown leisurely around each other,
perhaps in the bunkbed of the ship
my father sailed on, the small space
made even smaller by the presence of the two bodies,

their long peaceful breaths mingling as they dream.
That's Walt Whitman, I'd say, to anyone who'd listen and look,
and next to him, I'd add proudly, that's my father.

### 3. Teresa at the Piano

"Walt objected to the piano."
– Horace Traubel

I think he would have loved it
if he'd known my mother,
who played an upright at the heart
of all the parties she and my father threw
when I was growing up, the many guests
crowded in a semi-circle around her,
the spirit no doubt like that of Whitman's
Pfaff's, his Broadway hangout—the camaraderie,
the free-flowing talk and drink and food and song.

Whitman thought the sounds the piano made
were not fit for great music,
the instrument's timbre not hefty enough
for his beloved opera.
Writing his own sweeping lines, he could hear
behind and beneath him, in support,
orchestral music, never piano music.

How could he, who loved mothers,
not have loved her, and therefore loved
what came to life under her fingers,

her playing by ear perhaps a cousin to his free verse,
her rendering of pop tunes, Broadway favorites,
and sentimental Irish ballads surely an example
of America singing? And he'd have heard, amazed
at how wrong he'd been about the piano.

I want them to meet: Walt, Teresa; Mom, Walt.
For is he not in his nurturing
as much a mother as a father?
Oh, but I think now I am already too late,
and they have met as ghosts visiting St. Louis,
where she lived and he visited his brother,
and he has taken her hands into his
and noticed her long, slender fingers,
what she called her "piano fingers."
When he wrote, "Your mother....is she living?....
Have you been much with her? and has she been
much with you?" surely he was talking to me,
and for a brief moment my name
rises between them like a note
struck from a piano.

# EQUINE

## 1. Horses

They rode in the rain, father, daughter, son,
in Ireland, on horses rented
for an hour, but the rain would not relent
and soaked them to the skin.

To see them riding in the rain,
you could not tell their history—
a recent divorce, the trip a way
to ride beyond the deep pour of pain.

It was their last day on that isle.
Before they flew away, they simply had
to meet their long-planned goal: a ride
on horseback on ancestral Irish soil,

rain or no. As a horse gestures with a toss
of its mane, so did these gesture
by circling the wet, green pasture
in the aftermath of loss,

three united in their will to sit tall
in any weather, savoring the creak
and feel of leather atop a strong back
all muscle and hide, before farewell.

## 2. On a Photo of His Daughter

I'm moved to see you on a horse once more.
You look at home there, free of any care.

Behind you, Minnesota farmland runs
flat and far, your hands intimate with reins.

Though urban and urbane, you'd easily pass
for one who'd grown up deep in prairie grass—

or maybe for a female centaur, half
of you heavy brown flesh to hold you safe.

At thirty-six, you're somewhere in the middle
of your ride. Better than a throne, a saddle.

The horse's left eye is a darkened pool
where your future swims, gleaming like a jewel.

But this photo also brings a pang: that I
before long must bid you, Rider, goodbye.

Your sweet smile says, "I think I'll sit a while
longer here, it feels so right behind this pommel."

Horse, woman, daughter, farmland, tree line, sky—
each and all the answer to the question, Why?

# SISTERS

## 1. Family Report

*–for Ingrid*

The baby had her first fall, rolling off the bed.
She's fine. Let's hope in later years she fares as well—
With nothing but the normal painful tales to tell—
Falling not off the bed but on to it instead.

## 2. Arabesque: A Prayer

*–for Sorcha*

May my granddaughter's earliest memory
Be that of the day I taught her the arabesque.
An old heron, I wobbled on one leg, while she,
Four, made swift, light work of the artful task.

No better afterlife for me than in
Her mind, two arms in front, one leg behind.
In time may her imagination prove kind
And improve my amateur's technique. Amen.

# SEAMUS HEANEY: CENTO SONNET

at the New York Ethical Culture Society

There are heard melodies and h-e-r-d melodies.
My teachers never taught us poetry;
instead they gave us poems to memorize.
The most difficult rhetorical form for me
is the commencement address, especially
since optimism is not my strongest suit.
Hope's not optimism—"All will be all right"—
but takes root and blossoms when history
advances from atrocious to merely messy;
hope says, "There's work to be done, stick to it."
My own history in northern Ireland was fraught
with high voltage under decorousness. What
better definition of poetry could you have?
I'm still learning to read the poems I love.

# ON LEARNING IRISH HAS NO WORD FOR "YES" OR "NO"

In Irish I don't have to answer
"Is your brother dead?" with "Yes"
but can say, "He is, he is,"
and keep him alive in the predicate.

When you live in an occupied country,
you learn to be circumlocutious.
Yes or no is dangerous.
"Is this man your friend?"
"I've seen him here often."

A single word will never do
as long as there are three or four
to accomplish the same thing.
Let other languages take rock-solid
immobile stands, feet planted.
In Irish, the multiple steps perform
a jig in your ear.

Try it for a day—no yes or no.
Afterwards, I'll ask, "Did you like that?"
You can say, "It was refreshment for my brain,"
or, "My tongue might as well have been stone."

Nothing in nature so definite
as yes or no.
The moon and sun say maybe.
"Is this a poem?"
"You can call it what you want."

# PSALM FOR FAY

> "Dad, my dream is to marry a matador in Ireland
> and have a big Jewish wedding."

Behold, beside the waters of the River Liffey, I will give my daughter away as I wave a red cape at the groom.

Whereupon shall a bull lie down like a lamb amongst us, under the four-cornered indoor sky of our silken chuppah, his sweet and warm breath more powerful, yea, more appealing than incense, and his eyes as black as the blood pudding served for breakfast in the modest and welcoming homes of Westport, County Mayo.

Verily, the ghost of Fay's great-grandfather Owen McGinn, having come directly from his childhood home and current haunt, Cavan, and looking like Yahweh Himself, will usher astonished guests to their seats.

For I have seen the guest list, Lord, and it includes Leopold Bloom, who shall sing a song in praise of his wife, declaring her to be zaftig, and one for Woman herself, selected parts of Whom he will with great reverence name. Selah.

Blessed be the klezmer band and the musicians from Madrid's plaza de la corrida, united for this day, who will play what sounds like a cross between "Bei Mir Bist Du Schon," as interpreted by Sammy Cahn, and "Pasodoble," the toreadors' grand entrance march.

With gladness and rejoicing shall we jig, execute a veronica, or link arms and dance the hora around the Ark of the Covenant, here represented by a wedding cake in the shape of Yeats's tower at Ballylee.

As we do so, mark, ye Wasps, how we kick loose from our shoes sand from Tel Aviv, each grain the eye of history looking straight at you; industrial dust from the streets of Cork; and Andalusian clay, walked on by Lorca and still dreaming his dreams, like this wedding born of a Minnesota woman impregnated by a cosmic wind.

Therefore shall I take from my pocket, like a matador sliding a sword from its sheath, a handkerchief of one hundred per cent Irish linen and give it to the bride and groom to hold between their hands as they circle each other.

For the harp of Israel and the harp of the green isle shall be one.

As enthusiastically as townspeople carried Manolete in triumph through the squares of Cordoba and as easily as Buck Mulligan raised his bowl of lather in mockery of the sacred Host to begin the eternity of June 16, 1904, will eight banderilleros lift the bride and groom upon two chairs and sway them with tender mercies above the heads of the applauding congregation to the measures of "The Lass of Aughrim."

Let the glass goblet from which the bride and groom drink brim with Guinness, its lacy foam as pure as the dew that descended upon the mountains of Zion, and the groom stomp on the glass as the rabbi shouts, "Ole!" and "Slainte!"

Let the moment of truth upon this occasion be the taking of identical vows which, like sword blades flashing at five o'clock in the afternoon, doubly pierce the hearts of all fathers present.

And let Molly Bloom, even if she should arrive late and out of breath in a rush after concluding some necessary and herein tactfully unnamed business in Dublin, interpret, at least for her own purposes, the resounding "Amen" not as "So be it," which confirms the past, but as "Yes," which declares—as tables laden with steaming kosher corned beef and paella wait in the antechamber—an appetite for the future.

# TIN

He would go back to Africa
just to lie again
under a tin roof
and hear the rain,

and not just any rain
but in season,
rain like a river,
beyond reason,

its roar, as if the river
played its own drum,
enough to drown
her love-come

or the angry buzz
of some starved mosquito,
the netting all around them
ghostly in the glow

from the oil lamp lit
beside the narrow bed
that he might see her better,
only months his bride

and far from home,
although that sound
was theirs to live in
like a native land,

complete with sky
of corrugated tin
and torrent of lullaby,
which he would hear again.

## "BETWEEN WOMEN"

He loves the phrase,
so optimistic
and ambiguous—
suggesting either a temporary state of
womanlessness,
or a woman on either side of him,
two sisters, say, comfortable at sharing,
or even the two girls
dressed as guardian angels
in his first communion picture, each
a year older than he and at an elbow,
denying, by their garb and heavenly smiles
for the camera, their sex—unless,
of course, what's meant is
"before and after," as in
"source and issue," his mother and daughter,
although most likely
the phrase should be read as a way of saying
the earth itself, from which and into which,
the two women really one
and he not between them
but, except for a time
and like a faithful lover,
in her.

# GIRLFRIENDS

Tired of our wars,
I want to be one of your girlfriends,
a male girlfriend
with whom you have sex

but whom you also trust
like Mary or Judy or Jasmin or Ann.

We'll stay up late talking,
protective armor
strewn across the floor,
giggling cozily
in our permanent sleepover.

Battle of the sexes?
Good for a laugh, a ribald joke.

I'll slouch around
in an old nightgown,
something you were about to discard
that will hide my genitals
nicely for the time being.

I'll be the boyfriend
you talk about
to the girlfriend I've become
as I shake a knowing
and sympathetic head.

Men!

We'll pour drinks and toast ourselves:
girlfriends forever.

# VILLANELLE SEXTET

## 1. Treadmill

"In Shepherdstown, West Virginia, for the peace talks, Farouk al-Shara surprisingly accepted Ehud Barak's invitation to run on the treadmill next to him in the hotel gym."
– World Press Review, March, 2000

Syria's running miles in place next to Israel.
One foot up and one down's the way to peace.
They're going nowhere mile after mile.

Start slow is the plan, then a gradual
acceleration till a dove wins the race.
Syria's running side by side with Israel.

The machines rumble so, talking's minimal,
and what there is of it's not face-to-face.
Two countries go nowhere mile after mile.

Still, when Israel hands Syria a towel,
the Golan Heights seem doable, more or less,
Syria running neck-and-neck with Israel.

Nike fills the mediator's role,
and sweat's a lubricant, diplomacy's grease,
but the going stays tough, mile after mile.

Now the workout's ending. What better goal
than hot showers? In steam, soaped up, a truce.
Who's more out of breath? Syria or Israel?
Tomorrow another treadmill, mile after mile.

## 2. The Ice-Cream Vigils

> "Whitman managed to get hold of ten gallons of ice cream, which he personally dispensed to the patients at Carver Hospital."
> – Roy Morris, Jr., *The Better Angel*

Ice cream for a soldier, whether North or South.
Dispense it quickly, while it's at its best.
A spoon at a time, death melts in the mouth.

It's cold enough to make you catch your breath.
For some westerners, this was their first taste
of ice cream, the flavor neither North nor South,

perfect to smooth a battle's aftermath.
The war's real story—ask the seasoned journalist
from Brooklyn—melted spoon by spoon in the mouth,

a frozen treat become the whole of truth
while it was going down. How could it last
in June, in Washington, the winds warm from the south?

To serve mere boys who'd served away their youth,
Walt Whitman crossed the capital in haste
lest there be nothing left to melt in the mouth.

Ice-cream communion, lips parted in faith,
and the inclined head of a volunteer pagan priest—
scenario for healing North and South
a spoon at a time. Death melts in the mouth.

### 3. Eye-glasses

Phnom Penh, 1976

I throw away my glasses lest I die.
Can you wear glasses safely where you are?
Here, Khmer Rouge are killing the bourgeoisie.

Glasses mean books, which mean modernity,
which means the power to question those in power.
I throw away my glasses lest I die.

If I don't squint and act as if I see,
I may escape the guardians of the pure.
Khmer Rouge are murdering the bourgeoisie.

There's politics in wearing glasses. Why
not? The world's gone mad. Not yours? Are you sure?
I throw away my glasses lest I die.

To hide a university degree,
I simply render everything a blur.
Khmer Rouge are rooting out the bourgeoisie.

You're free to wear glasses? What a luxury!
So read a book while you can. I'll play laborer
and throw away my glasses lest I die.
Here, Khmer Rouge are killing the bourgeoisie.

### 4. Brady

"On the ornate gold clock Brady frequently used as a prop in his pictures, the time was always 11:52."
– *Mathew Brady: His Life and Photographs*, George Sullivan

The time is always eleven-fifty-two
in Brady's studio. Forenoon? Foremidnight?
If time has stopped, whatever are we to do?

Lincoln today, tomorrow Whitman. A who's who
of subjects. But no one can set the clock right.
The time is always eleven-fifty-two.

The dead lie free of time, whether grey or blue;
a dead clock's hands can't move and spoil a shot.
If time's not moving, what then of me and you?

In Brady's war photographs, the dead strew
the battlefield perfectly; he saw to that.
When you move a corpse, it's eleven-fifty-two.

His Broadway studio's clock says, "Just a few
more minutes, then I'll ring the hour out."
It's civil, this warning. But what are we to do?

Brady posed both live and dead and knew
no matter what the clock says, Civil War or not,
the time is always even-fifty-two.
There's only one time: it's now, for me and you.

### 5. The Lifeguard

Grey day, the water all ice, no swimmers there,
the beach deserted as I come running by,
but someone's sitting in the lifeguard's chair.

I do a double-take, slow down, and stare.
He's a still, dark silhouette against the sky.
Cold, grey day, the water's ice, no swimmers anywhere.

Although the hand of someone gasping for air
is not about to wave and catch his eye,
there's someone sitting in the lifeguard's chair.

The Prince of Ice? Lord of the Land of Despair?
Or, off-season, someone missing work, his perch on high,
now that snow's back, no swimmers anywhere?

Or maybe it's himself he'd save, aware
of ways men drown that aren't so watery,
and so he's come to try the lifeguard's chair.

And now I think I know him, as in a mirror.
Alone and distant. At a remove. So sit I.
Cold, grey day, the water's ice, no swimmers there,
though someone's sitting in the lifeguard's chair.

### 6. The Upright Piano

They're moving a piano into 604.
I see the upright coming down the street.
Will I hear Bach or Broadway through the floor?

My mother played an upright year after year
in our dining room as if music were something to eat.
They're moving a piano into 604.

Now the upright's in the elevator
like an arpeggio of rising note after note.
Will I hear Chopin or ragtime through the floor?

In my dream the apartment building's no mere
building now but alive, a body with a heartbeat
at its center—the piano in 604.

My mother played for party guests by ear,
pop tunes and Irish standards. She was a hit.
Will I hear the "Rose of Tralee" through the floor?

Maybe scales, a child stepping up onto the first stair.
Or an improvisation, how we play our lives out.
They're moving a piano into 604.
What news—sharp, flat, major, minor—through the floor?

# MACHETE

> "The rebels in Sierra Leone relegated 10,000 people
> to life without arms, legs, ears, even lips."
> – Reuters

We take pains with our work. Our stamp
of excellence? Professional-looking stumps.

And we refuse to be rushed. After all,
you'll be our walking advertisements—well,

our choice of words may be unfortunate
but we know you'll relish your fate

at our hands. Your ears are easily removed—
just two strokes of the whistling blade.

Arms and legs require a bit more work.
Lips, though, are the highest test of our technique.

They must be pulled forward, the head held down
to a flat surface where the lower first can

be pressed. Angle, of course, is everything,
and speed: our instrument's a flashing wing.

Then the upper—careful to bend the nose
to the side—and, voila, the mouth is a rose.

Our complete package leaves you a citizen
of the modern world, a bundle of sleek skin,

no unnecessary protuberances
to get caught in machines, no more chances

you'll feel power's corrupting pull.
Rebels? We're artists. Look: you're beautiful.

# RELIGIONE AL DENTE

> "The new Tooth Relic Pagoda holds a tooth said
> to have belonged to the Buddha."
> – The Dharma Times (Aug.,2009)

I might have stayed with my childhood faith
if I could now be attending
the Church of the Holy Cavity
or the Wisdom Tooth Basilica.

I imagine Dr. Etzkorn, my dentist
as priest, conducting the ritual of a saviour
nailed to the cross of periodontal disease
while, at the Church of the Missing Molar,
the relic works its miracles in absentia.

If only my religion could have had
a patron saint of braces
and my hand been able to swim
in a holy water font treated
with fluoride and chlorophyll.
If we are what we eat,
the teeth cut close to the soul,
redemption as whitened enamel.

Better a baby tooth of Jesus
in a chapel in Rome
than the Shroud of Turin.
For communion wafer,
the little cardboard square
I bite down on as the dental assistant
disappears behind a buzz of radiation.

To protect myself I make this sign:
in the name of the Overbite
and of the Loose Tooth
and of the Yellowed Incisor.

# COLD

## 1. Thaw

The ice beside the lake has something to say.
Its crackling static puzzles me as I pass.
Or else it's talking to itself. Or ice
is many and a meeting's underway:
on the agenda, cold and melt and how to move
as water. I see I need to take a class
in speaking Ice so I could ask advice
on how to master changing lest I prove
to be rock-solid frozen for all my days
to come, one-seasoned, heated air or no.
Ice, a hard self all winter, now lets go
and disappears, transformed. Maybe it's praise
I heard—ice feeling fortunate to die
into water—and then the Ice word for goodbye.

## 2. The Saint of Winter

Like a child, I hate winter clothes.
I want the weather my way.
This tangle of sleeves and layers,
buttons and strings—God, how I thrash
(now I've made things worse), crazy to be free!

But elsewhere, another, or so I suppose,
curbs his will to dress for the cold day,
each slow, patient move a prayer.
His face nearly interred in a mask,
he does not strain even to see.

# REBUILDINGS

Hennepin County Medical Center, Minneapolis

Outside, the Vikings stadium; inside, my blood.
Destroy, create; rebuilding on the old site.
Cranes hoist my healthy white blood cells sky high
when chemotherapy throws a Hail Mary pass.
My brother, the Vikings stadium. Who would guess?
I hear the ghosts of tiers of future fans
cheering a fourth-quarter goal-line stand in my veins:
the Leukemia Lions versus the Chemo Kings.
Under every hard hat, a good white blood cell
and each proud to be carrying a union card;
the bad ones support every right-to-work law.
Are those cell counts or touchdowns on the scoreboard?
Bulldozers build up a steep bank of hemoglobin
as doctors huddle, strategize for a first down.

## LIBRARY

They're tearing down the library.
They'll build another in its place,
but now they're tearing down the library.

Large machines are eating the library.
The books have fled.
The books are refugees.

The reading rooms are open to the wind.
You can check out the wind now
at the checkout desk.

A steam shovel scoops up
a great mound of earth like someone
devouring a book in one sitting.

Readers stand outside the chainlink fence.
They read anything they can. They read the dust
of pulverized stone that blows their way.

The site will lie idle during the winter.
The snow will pile, flecked by grit,
looking like a shelf of old newspapers.

A crow lands. The new librarian.
It calls out Dewey decimal numbers
in its own dark language.

# EMMETT'S STORY

In one of his poems, long before he died,
my father had written that heaven for him would be
driving forever through the cosmos in
a car with his three children for company—
inside, precious conversations; outside,
galaxy after galaxy, and deep space.

Not that he loved driving for its own sake,
he emphatically didn't. What he loved
was the uninterrupted and distraction-free
time with us, the sense of intimacy
and focus in such an enclosed environment.

So that when he lay dying in the hospital,
with only days or hours remaining, we—
my brother and sister and I—conceived the scheme
of springing him from his room and driving him
from town to town and through the countryside,
engaged with him one last time, until he died.

Late that night, while Fay kept the nurses on duty
on my father's floor tied up at their desk answering
question after question, most visitors gone,
Austin and I, after dropping on the nightstand
an explanatory note begging forgiveness
and understanding from the staff, draped
our father's arms around our shoulders and hoisted
him up out of bed, then carried him, his toes
skimming along the floor like a ballet dancer's,

to the freight elevator around the corner from
his room and which at that time of night was idle.
We'd earlier cased the route and soon had him
in the parking lot, where Fay met us with the car.

Although we'd told him in his room we wanted
to take him for a drive and he'd nodded and smiled,
I wasn't sure he understood as we eased
him into the back seat and—Fay beside him, Austin
at the wheel—drove away from Mayo and out
of Rochester. But when, with the countryside
surrounding us, my siblings and I agreed
the darkness we drove through was itself like deep space,
our car the cosmic vehicle of his poem,
my father, pointing to a farmyard's light
atop a sky-tall pole, quietly joined in
the serious game: "And there's a star to prove it."

As the towns passed—Blue Earth, Owatonna, Waldorf—
we stopped from time to time to switch drivers and
take turns in the back seat so that each of us
had our moments with him in between his naps,
talking of a dish he cooked, say; a house he owned;
but especially what we remembered of
childhood trips with him—Mexico, Ireland, Spain—
each of which now somehow seemed preparation
for this one. But all of that was before the deer.

The deer was in the middle of the road
just as I came around a bend and caught
him in my headlights. I hit the breaks and stopped

ten feet from him. He stood and didn't scare
but only stared, motionless, straight at the car,
as if he could see past the headlights and into
the darkness where we were. He looked long
and long, like one thinking, figuring something out.
I wasn't sure who was more in the spotlight,
he or the four of us. When he'd seen and thought
enough, he snorted. Then snorted again. Whatever
they meant, his snorts were impossible to translate.
Letting us go, he lowered his head and turned
away, unhurried, and walked out of our lights.

"What did you make of that, Dad?" Austin asked.
But he was asleep, and we went on. His sleep,
however, was permanent, we shortly discovered.
I pulled over, stopped the car, and killed the engine,
and we opened all the doors—I don't know why—
and stood on the shoulder of the road awhile.

Returning the body to the hospital,
we were spotted en route and sirened to a halt
by the state patrol, who'd been alerted by Mayo.
One officer checked my father while the other
questioned us and wrote down our story. The two
were business-like, citing various possible
violations, but then escorted us the rest
of the way; no charges were ever pressed. Still, after
that night, we took to calling what we did
a caper. My father would have liked that word.

# Afterword

Letter to a Young Poet:

Stay young. I mean: enact a permanent apprenticeship. Never arrive if arrival means a comfortable place—a way of writing, a manner. Why imitate yourself? Let others do that. Remember Picasso's answer to the charge that he lacked a single, identifiable style: "Does God have a style?" His answer's arrogance doesn't vitiate its point. The poet, no homebody, takes up residence only on "the open road"; even (especially) Emily Dickinson, despite all appearances to the contrary, was never at home.

One way to preserve a certain innocence: keep your distance from Jeffers' "thickening center." The literary network may be less a system of communication lines than a web that entangles. Just make the poems and trust in the universe that what you write will find its audience without your shepherding it overly. What matters is that you're at work in the vineyard where greats have worked, and it's a privilege to bend to the task in the presence of such ghosts. And if all you've written turns finally to mere mulch, through which other work will later grow, consider yourself part of that flourishing-to-come. Frost had it right: "What's worth succeeding in is worth failing in." As indentured servitudes go, the life of poetry can't be beat.

By the way, no one owes you anything. Expect rejections. You needn't love them, but think of the boxer—does he enjoy getting hit? Well, no, but, still, he loves boxing, and getting hit is part of it. Welcome the rough-and-tumble of your independence; let schmoozers have their soft life.

Wish for your pen the approximation of a state of perpetual motion. Writer's blocks are inventions of people who want to claim the glamour of the writing life but are not willing to sweat on schedule; so they put on the mantle of suffering heroes. As such poseurs bewail their fate, respond by simply meeting your obligation: scribble on.

The above originally appeared in *The Midwest Quarterly: A Journal of Contemporary Thought* (Summer, 2003), a special issue devoted to poets' "Letters to Young Poets."

## About the Author

A native of St. Louis, Philip Dacey earned master's degrees from Stanford and the University of Iowa Writer's Workshop. A Sixties Peace Corps volunteer in Nigeria, he taught at Miles College, Birmingham, Alabama, during the presidency of Dr. Lucius Pitts. From 1970 until his retirement in 2004 he taught at Southwest Minnesota State University in Marshall, On leaves of absence, he lived for six months in Spain with his wife and their two children and later lived in Mexico for five months with his wife and their three children. Besides making several trips to his ancestral Ireland and one to Vietnam along with various veterans, students, and colleagues, a 1995 Fulbright brought him to Yugoslavia for four months. Upon his retirement in 2004, he moved to Manhattan's Upper West Side for a post-retirement adventure. With Alixa Doom, his partner since 2001, he lived in the lake district of Minneapolis from 2012 until his death in 2016.

## Goodbye, Dear Friend

Dear Phil,

I want to get some things said to you before they turn into elegies. From our days as young profs at Southwest, then the long spatial but only in miles separation, and then a renewed closeness when you were in NYC, you have always been a person of great importance to me. How lucky to have you as a friend in Minnesota when I was hungry for poetry companionship and knowledge (which I had at Syracuse and thought I wouldn't have again), and there you were, better educated than I and such a fine fellow (however Catholic tortured) and how we hit it off right away. All that's history now, but significant to me. I know I would not have become the poet I think I am without your presence as a poet and as a man.

I especially love how you embraced Barbara after my divorce, and our times together in New York, our dinners, and trips to Julliard, and our many discussions about writing and more, and how Barbara came to know your worth to me, and finally to her. So time is on my mind, almost 50 years of it. The intelligence you have brought to my poems over the years has been invaluable. I will miss it terribly. Your best poems, the long ones in particular, will be your afterlife, and I will do my best to keep them alive. I'm also pleased how much I've come to like Alixa, and doubly pleased by her love and admiration for you, and how she has enriched for you these last few years.

Thank you for your years of kindness and attention.

Love,
Stephen

Stephen Dunn is Distinguished Professor of Creative Writing at Richard Stockton College of New Jersey

## Acknowledgments

These poems have appeared in the following journals as indicated:

*The Asses of Parnassus*: The D Minor Organ Toccata and Fugue
*Big City Lit*: For Aunt Mary, Who Jumped; Treadmill, Rondel for Bernard
*Bryant Literary Review*: Zoot: A Rondel
*The Cafe Review*: Black and White
*California Quarterly*: Walking the Picket Line With the Ghosts of My Father and Grandfather
*Clare*: On Learning Irish Has No Word for "Yes" or "No"
*Common Ground Review*: Seamus Heaney: Cento Sonnet
*The Cortland Review*: The Saint of Winter
*Eureka Literary Magazine*: "Between Women"
*The Falcon*: In Praise of Chinese Pottery
*Fox Chase Review*: On a Photo of His Daughter, Shower: A Triolet
*Grey Sparrow Journal*: Horses
*Hanging Loose*: Girlfriends
*The Hopkins Review*: Walt and Joe
*Innisfree Poetry Journal*: Teresa at the Piano
*Kerf*: Ice Cream Vigils
*The Laurel Review*: Machete
*The Lyric*: Bic
*Measure: A Review of Formal Poetry*: The Upright Piano, Song of the Hat Vendor, City: On the Photography of Doug Johnson
*Minnetonka Review*: The Buzz
*Nightsun*: Tin
*North American Review*: First Memory, Leaves of Lucre, Religione al Dente
*Northern Student*: O Dad Untie the Knot!

*Pemmican*: Letter to Thomas McGrath; Eye-glasses
*The Prose Poem: An International Journal*: Psalm for Fay
*Red Booth Review*: "What Do You Miss Most About New York City?"
*River Oak Review*: Saratoga Springs
*Skidrow Penthouse*: Piano
*Slant*: Emmett's Story; Library; The Lifeguard; Fellini at Lake Calhoun (Minneapolis)
*Southern Poetry Review*: Thaw, Brady
*Southwest Journal*: Rebuildings
*Tampa Review*: The Answer
*Tar River Poetry*: The Pugilists, Not About Pie Thieves, Family Report
*Third Wednesday*: Fly
*Water~Stone Review*: Manhattan Song

"Leaves of Lucre" received Honorable Mention for the 2009 James Hearst Poetry Prize from the *North American Review*. "Manhattan Song" was reprinted as a bookmark by *Water~Stone Review*. "Girlfriends" was reprinted in *The Great American Poetry Show* (The Muse Media, 2015). "Letter to Thomas McGrath" was reprinted in *Eating the Pure Light: Homage to Thomas McGrath* (Backwaters Press, 2009).